Budget Cooking for One

Supper Dishes

Budget Recipes for One – The Art of Cooking for Yourself

DISCLAIMER

All information in the book is for general information purposes only.

The author has used her best efforts in preparing this information and makes no representations or warranties with respect to the accuracy, applicability or completeness of the material contained within.

Furthermore, the author takes no responsibility for any errors, omissions or inaccuracies in this document. The author disclaims any implied or expressed warranties or fitness for any particular purpose.

The author shall in no event be held liable for losses or damages whatsoever. The author assumes no responsibility or liability for any consequences resulting directly or indirectly from any action or lack of action that you take based on the information in this document.

Use of the publication and recipes therein is at your own risk.

Reproduction or translation of any part of this publication by any means, electronic or mechanical, without the permission of the author, is both forbidden and illegal. You are not permitted to share, sell, and trade or give away this document and it is for your own personal use only, unless stated otherwise.

By using any of the recipes in this publication, you agree that you have read the disclaimer and agree with all the terms.

The reader assumes full risk and responsibility for all actions taken as a result of the information contained

Table of Contents

Introduction

After raising a family of five sons alone I found it extremely difficult to adjust to cooking for one when they all left home. I still found myself peeling a mountain of potatoes and vegetables or cooking a very large portion of rice or pasta even though I was dining alone.

I also found it hard to shop for one; I had to stop myself from buying a huge cut of meat, a large loaf of bread and a huge carton of milk. It was a real eye opener when I eventually got the hang of being a one person household. My shopping habits changed and cooking became fun when I realized I was able to buy only things I liked to cook and eat. The other good thing was the money I could save by buying in smaller amounts.

The difficult bit was finding good, tasty budget recipes to try my hand at. So I did a lot of research and testing and wrote down my results and recipes for future reference. Once I had a good selection of recipes I sent them to my children who were at college.

All my boys are good cooks and can produce a great meal – much to the amazement of their friends. The recipes in this book are all tried and tested by me and my children and not taken from random websites.

After checking out a lot of cookery books I realized that not a lot of books cater for single people; either students living alone, career people who prefer not to eat convenience 'TV' dinners, older people who like to cook and bake but don't because they invariably end up wasting a lot of the food they cook or can't afford to buy the expensive ingredients that are suggested in the 'celebrity' cookery books.

I watched a lot of the cookery programs on TV and, although the food looks great, the ingredients were always high end stuff. For example, Jamie Oliver has a TV series and cookbook called '15 Minute Meals' which was very interesting but, unless you have a large grocery budget and very well stocked store cupboard, most of the recipes will definitely break the bank. I know I couldn't afford to buy T bone steaks and truffles, even if I could make a tasty meal in 15 minutes...

I can never understand people who say they don't have time to cook.

Most of the recipes in this book can be prepared for the oven in less than 10 minutes. So, as my kids say, 'it's a no brainer' to cook for myself; I know exactly what is going into my food and it is so much more tasty.

In the following pages you will find 45 recipes that are simple to make, are designed either for one meal for one person or are recipes that can be easily divided and frozen for another day. Throughout this book you will see this:

Suitable for
Vegetarian

This tells you that a particular recipe is either a vegetarian recipe or can easily be adapted to vegetarian.

The ingredients are easy to find and usually cheap to buy. A lot of the recipes show interesting ways to use left-overs too. Where possible I have used fresh, seasonal produce unless there is a good alternative. For example, I would never spend time shelling peas (life is too short...) when I have a bag of frozen peas in the freezer.

I would encourage you to be creative and add extras to the recipes. You may have vegetables that need using up so add them to your dish. Add different herbs and spices to see what tastes good to you. Have fun cooking!

I hope this 'Cooking for One' cookery book helps you to create interesting, cheap and mouthwatering meals that you will enjoy eating.

Store Cupboard Essentials

Your store cupboard will, over time, come to contain many of the ingredients you will need to try a new recipe.

Make it a habit to buy one item to add to your store cupboard each time you go to the supermarket. That way it won't cost a fortune but you will quickly build up a stash of staple ingredients for lots of recipes.

Another thing that I have started to do is to grow some herbs in a window box on the kitchen windowsill. I grow chives, parsley, coriander and oregano at the moment and intend to grow more. It's really easy – even for a house plant killer such as myself...

Below is a list of things that I routinely have in my store cupboard but you may have other ingredients that you want to add.

Seasonings

Sea Salt
Black pepper
White pepper
Dried Herbs
Dried Spices
Dried Chili
Mustard Powder

Cans

Tomatoes
Tuna
Peanut Butter
Coconut Milk
Beans – baked beans, butter beans, kidney beans etc.

Bottles

Honey
Vinegar
Red or (and) White Wine Vinegar
Vegetable oil
Olive Oil
Extra Virgin Olive Oil
Tomato Ketchup
Soy Sauce
Worcestershire Sauce
Mustard
Chopped Garlic

Dry Stuff

Flour
Pasta
Oats
Rice
Noodles
Stock Cubes
Dried Mushrooms

Fridge

Crème Fraiche
Eggs
Milk
Cheese

Freezer

Vegetables – Peas, Green Beans, Sweetcorn
etc.
Berries – Raspberries, Strawberries,
Gooseberries etc.
Bread – Part Baked and Sliced Shop Bought

Don't underestimate the usefulness of your
freezer. These days frozen vegetables are
just as nutritious as fresh ones and bread
can be taken and used one or two slices at a
time. You may also need to freeze any
leftover soups and recipes you have made
and divided to save for another day.

It is so easy to get stuck in a rut and make
the same few meals over and over. So try
and vary your meals by compiling a weekly
menu, making a list of the ingredients you
will need and shopping at the beginning of
each week.

You will begin to look forward to mealtimes
when you know that you will be having
something different, nutritious, quick and
simple to make and exactly to your own
taste.

Remember, variety is the spice of life and you should make sure that a lot of your variety is in your diet.

Supper Dishes

The following pages contain a selection of tried and tested supper dishes that are easy to prepare, economical and very tasty. An added bonus is that many of them are easily adaptable so you can add your own favorite ingredients.

Shepherds Pie

This dish is an ideal meal for when the weather is cold and wet. For me it is the ultimate 'comfort food'. When I make this I usually make two and pop one in the freezer for another day; it freezes well.

Ingredients

250g minced (ground) beef
1 onion
1 carrot
Flour or cornflour for thickening
2 or 3 large potatoes.
Handful of grated Cheddar cheese (optional)
Salt and pepper

Method

Put the minced beef in a saucepan and cover with plenty of water. Break up the meat whilst bringing it to the boil. When it is boiling take a large spoon and skim the 'scum' from the top of the pan – this is fat. When you have skimmed as much fat as you can from the minced meat, finely chop the onion and carrot and add to the pan.

Bring back to the boil then turn the heat down until it is just bubbling a little. Simmer until the onion and carrot are soft. Mix a little cornflour with cold water then add to the simmering minced beef to thicken the gravy; don't make it too thick.

Taste and add salt and pepper to your liking.

Put the minced beef into a colander to separate the gravy from the meat then divide the meat between two ovenproof dishes. Using a colander rather than a sieve allows some of the gravy to pass through, keeping the meat nice and moist. Keep the remaining gravy to one side for serving.

Peel and chop the potatoes into small even sized chunks and bring to the boil. Turn the heat down and simmer until cooked. Once cooked drain the water off, season with salt and white pepper then mash with a little butter or milk. You don't want the potatoes too soft.

Layer the mashed potatoes over the minced beef, finishing off with a fork to level the dish. Sprinkle with the cheese. You could also add a few pieces of thinly sliced tomatoes if you like. Put one under the grill until the top is golden brown. The other can be frozen for another day.

Serve with vegetables and the gravy that you put aside.

Quick Beetroot Soup

Simple to make and a favorite of mine.

Ingredients

2 Cooked Beetroots
1 Carrot
1 Onion
1 Stick of Celery
½ pint Vegetable Stock
Small knob of Butter
Seasoning

Method

Cut up and cook carrot, onion and celery in the vegetable stock until soft. Grate the beetroot and add to the pan keeping a little back to add later for a bit of texture. Simmer for 2 minutes until the cooked beetroot is hot.

Put your soup in a blender and blitz to the desired consistency adding extra stock if needed.

Taste and season.

Put back in saucepan with the rest of the

grated beetroot to reheat. Add butter and stir well.

Serve with a swirl of cream or crème fraîche and some warm crusty bread – delicious!

Healthy Burgers

Burgers were always a particular favorite of my children but I was not happy buying the frozen variety. These Healthy Burgers are very quick to make and I usually make quite a few and freeze for later.

Ingredients

250g minced (ground) beef
I onion
Small amount of oil

Optional

Handful of grated cheese
Or
Clove of garlic
Or
1 red pepper
Or
A selection of vegetables

Method

Dice the onion (and garlic if you are using it) and fry in the oil until soft and translucent. I always soften the onions before adding to the meat to make sure they are cooked through. Put to one side. If using vegetables fry these until soft. Drain the oil off and discard. Allow the vegetables to cool slightly.

Place all your chosen ingredients in a large bowl with the minced beef and cooked onions and mix together well.

Shape into discs and put onto a lightly greased baking tray.

Cook in oven on 180c for about 20 minutes or until well cooked.

These burgers are great when served with a green salad or on a crusty roll.

Only cook the amount you want to eat and individually wrap and freeze the rest.

| Suitable for Vegetarian | *Potato Patties* |

These potato patties are great for using up left-over mashed potatoes and vegetables. They will freeze well and are a great accompaniment for bacon or sausages for a satisfying lunch.

Ingredients

Left over mashed potatoes
Any left-over vegetables
Flour
1 beaten egg
Butter and olive oil to cook.

Optional

Handful of grated cheese

Method

Put potatoes in large bowl, add beaten egg and vegetables (optional; will be just as nice plain). Mix together thoroughly.

Add enough flour to bring the mixture to a firm dough.

Divide into patties about 4 inches across and as thick as you want them to be.

Shallow fry until golden brown on both sides. Excellent for Sunday Brunch served with bacon or sausage and baked beans.

You can also add a handful of finely chopped herbs to liven up the potatoes.

Wrap any surplus patties individually and freeze for later.

Note: Try frying some bacon until crispy and add instead of vegetables – another treat for breakfast.

| Suitable for Vegetarian | *Mushroom Risotto* |

This is a very simple recipe and the mushroom can be replaced with anything you happen to have in the fridge. You could add left-over chicken or left-over vegetables or a handful of herbs.

Ingredients

Tablespoon of olive oil
Knob of butter
Small onion
1 clove of garlic
Hot Stock (chicken or vegetable)
120g Risotto rice
Small handful of frozen garden peas (optional)
Mushrooms (a small amount is fine)
Small handful of Parmesan or any grated cheese.
Salt and pepper

Method

Heat the oil and butter in a frying pan and add the onions and garlic. Fry gently until the onion is transparent and soft. Stir in the mushrooms and cook for a few minutes. If using cooked chicken, it will prevent the chicken drying out if you don't add until the rice is almost cooked.

Add the risotto rice and stir until the rice is well combined with the vegetables, butter and oil.

Begin to add the stock, a ladleful at a time, stirring thoroughly. Stir until the stock is absorbed before adding more. Keep adding the stock a ladleful at a time until the rice is soft but with a little bite. The risotto should be creamy.

Remove from heat, add peas if using, stir well and season. Serve immediately sprinkling with the grated cheese just before eating.

One Pan Breakfast Omelet

Ideal for supper or breakfast. Double the quantities to share with your friends.

Cooks altogether in one pan so saves on washing up – always a good thing according to my kids!

Ingredients

1 or 2 eggs
1 sausage
1 rasher back bacon
1 Tomato and mushroom
(optional)
Sliced red pepper
(optional)
Dessertspoon of milk
Small amount of oil for
cooking
Seasoning

Method

Cook sausage and bacon in the oil in a small frying pan. Remove from pan and chop into bite sized pieces. Cook tomato, mushroom and pepper if used. Set aside.

Beat the egg and milk together well, add seasoning.

Pour into the hot frying pan then return the sausage, bacon, tomato, mushroom and pepper to the pan. Swirl the egg mixture around the pan until it starts to cook. Allow to cook until the underside of the omelet is golden brown. Flip the omelet and cook for a further minute or two.

Alternatively, instead of flipping your omelet you can pop the pan under a hot grill to cook the top.

Serve immediately with baked beans and a slice of hot toast. Delicious!

Easy Spaghetti Bolognese

No need for a jar of ready-made sauce where you would waste half when making half portions – it's just as simple to make your own sauce designed just how you like it.

To make a vegetarian option substitute the minced beef for mushrooms and tomatoes.

Ingredients

250g minced (ground) beef
I small onion
Small amount of oil
Can of chopped tomatoes
Garlic
Any herbs you like
Mushrooms (optional)
Small red chili, chopped (optional)

Spaghetti
Black pepper for seasoning

Optional

Grated parmesan cheese

Method

Fry the onion, chopped chili and garlic if using, gently in the oil until soft and transparent. Add the minced beef, break up and fry for a few minutes until brown.

Pour in the can of chopped tomatoes and bring to the boil. Turn the heat down and simmer for 10 minutes to cook the minced beef. Add extra water if the pan is drying out.

Add any herbs you want – basil or oregano is very tasty. Stir well, taste and season to your liking.

Whilst the sauce is cooking add your spaghetti to a large saucepan of boiling water and cook until soft but still with a bit of 'bite'. Pour into a colander to drain liquid then pour over some boiling water to prevent the spaghetti from sticking together.

Put the spaghetti in a large bowl and add the sauce. Toss until all the spaghetti is coated. Tip onto your serving plate then garnish with grated parmesan and a few fresh herbs.

Serve with a few pieces of hot garlic bread.

Garlic Bread

This is an easy and delicious way to use up any bread that is going a bit hard or rolls that have been around for a day or two.

Ingredients

Couple of slices of crusty bread
Garlic
Good olive oil

Method

Place bread in frying pan with oil and fry on both sides until crisp and golden.
Remove from pan and rub peeled garlic over both sides whilst still quite warm.
Or
Take about 50g butter add crushed the garlic and mix together well.
Make cuts along a crusty roll, not quite cutting through. Insert the garlic butter in the cuts and place in medium oven for about 5 minutes.

| Suitable for Vegetarian | *Simple Homemade Pizza* |

This simple pizza can be prepared in a few minutes. You can use up ingredients that you already have in your fridge and store cupboard. For example, most people will have tomato ketchup in the cupboard so you don't need to buy tomato puree and there are usually a few tomatoes and bits of cheese that need using up. Left over vegetables are great to use too. Be inventive!

Ingredients

1 packet of frozen puff pastry
Tomato puree or tomato ketchup
Grated cheese
Topping of your choice
Few basil leaves (optional)

Method

Defrost puff pastry and cut in two. Wrap and refreeze one half for another time.

Roll out the puff pastry to around the thickness of a coin – square or circle; it doesn't matter. Place onto a baking tray.

Draw a line around the edge of your pastry base with a sharp knife about 1 inch from the edge without cutting through the pastry.

Squeeze about 2 inches of tomato puree or tablespoon of tomato ketchup onto the center of the base and spread evenly up to the scored line using the back of a spoon.

Add grated cheese then your choice of topping. Tomatoes, ham and leftover vegetables are my favorite. Sprinkle with a little more cheese and the basil leaves (if used).

Cook in the middle of oven using the temperature guide on the pastry packet. Cook until the pastry is crisp and golden around the edge of your pizza. Drizzle a little extra virgin olive oil over the pizza and serve immediately.

Note: You could use pitta bread for the pizza base if you prefer a crispy pizza. Simply open up the pitta bread and use as above.

Although this recipe is for tomato soup, you can use this method to make mushroom, vegetable, parsnip, broccoli or leek and potato soup. Simply omit the sugar from the tomato soup recipe and cook vegetables until soft.

Ingredients

6 medium tomatoes
Milk or mixture of milk and cream
1 clove garlic
Olive oil
1 teaspoon sugar
Salt and pepper
Herbs if desired
Grated cheese for serving

Method

Coat the tomatoes in the olive oil and place on baking tray. Crush the garlic and add to the tray along with any herbs you may be using. Shake the tray a few times before placing in the middle of a hot oven to roast – about 15 minutes.

Remove from oven and tip everything into a blender. Add the sugar and a little bit of milk and blitz. Keep adding the milk until your soup reaches the desired consistency. Put into saucepan and reheat. Taste and season.

Pour into bowl and sprinkle a little grated cheese over the top if using or you could swirl a spoonful of cream through the soup before serving. Serve with garlic croutons.

Note: Garlic croutons are quick and easy to make. Cut left over bread into small even squares. Crush and fry one clove of garlic in butter until softened. Add a little more butter along with the cubes of bread and fry gently on all sides until crisp and golden. Drain on kitchen paper. These croutons will freeze for use later. I always have a tub of croutons in the freezer.

Spiced Fried Chicken

The fun in this dish is combining spices to add to the breadcrumbs. Try lots of different combinations to find your favorite.

Ingredients

2 tablespoons of plain flour
Salt and black pepper
2 chicken portions
1 small egg
50g fresh white breadcrumbs
Spices of your choice
15g unsalted butter
3 tablespoons vegetable oil

Method

Put flour into large polythene bag and season. Add chicken and shake until the chicken is coated. Remove chicken and shake off excess flour.

Beat egg in a shallow bowl. Spread breadcrumbs on a plate – at this stage you could add any spice that you fancy to the breadcrumbs and combine well.

Dip the floured chicken in the egg and coat with the spiced (if you have added spices) breadcrumbs.

Melt the oil and butter in a frying pan over a medium to high heat. Add the chicken and fry for around 8-10 minutes each side or until the coating is golden brown and the chicken is cooked. Remove from pan and drain on kitchen paper. Serve immediately with a side of French fries or a crisp green salad.

You can have fun creating your own spiced breadcrumb mix – you never know, you could come up with some competition for KFC!!

Devilled Egg Salad Supper

A lovely, quick to prepare, light supper to eat in front of the TV.

Ingredients

2 eggs
Mayonnaise
Knob of butter
Dash of Worcestershire sauce
Paprika (or grated gruyere cheese)

Your choice of salad ingredients, for example:

Watercress
Tomatoes
Chopped peppers
Rocket leaves
Sweetcorn
Salad dressing
Etc..

Method

Put the eggs in a saucepan of cold water and boil for around 8 minutes. Drain and place eggs into a bowl of cold water.

When cold remove the shells and, using a sharp knife, cut each egg in half lengthways. Scoop the yolks out into a bowl. Add butter, mayonnaise (I quite often substitute the mayonnaise for salad cream) and

Worcestershire sauce. Mix together using a fork until smooth and well combined.

Spoon the mixture back into the egg whites and sprinkle with paprika (I sometimes omit the paprika and use a bit of grated gruyere cheese and melt under the grill).

Serve with your salad and a wedge of buttered crusty bread.

Switch on your favorite TV program and enjoy.

Easy Creamy Tuna Omelet

Everyone has a can of tuna lurking in the back of the store cupboard. Here is a tasty way to use it.

Ingredients

2 fresh eggs
Knob of butter
Small can of tuna chunks in oil
Tablespoon of chopped mushrooms
Tablespoon of frozen sweetcorn
50g Greek-style yoghurt
Salt and pepper

Method

Whisk eggs, add salt and pepper.

Drain the oil from the can of tuna into an omelet pan. Add mushrooms and sweetcorn, fry for 2 minutes. Add tuna and fry for a further minute. Stir in the yoghurt and cook until warmed through.

Remove mixture from pan and keep warm.

Wipe the pan with kitchen paper then melt the butter over a medium heat. Add the beaten eggs. Cook for around 3 minutes or until set. Remember not to stir or the eggs will scramble but occasionally draw in the edge with a wooden spatula to allow any uncooked egg to run underneath.

Top one half of the omelet with the tuna mixture. Fold over to enclose the filling. Serve immediately with a green salad or a few French fries.

Another tasty supper dish that can be prepared in about 15 minutes.

Ingredients

Tagliatelle for one
1 shallot
1 clove garlic
200g small tomatoes
100g savoy cabbage
1 tablespoon olive oil
2 tablespoons stock – chicken or vegetable
100g ricotta cheese
2 tablespoons cream
Grated cheese to garnish – if required

Method

Cook the pasta according to packet instructions, drain and keep warm.

Meanwhile finely chop the shallots, finely shred the cabbage, peel and crush garlic and cut tomatoes into quarters.

Heat oil in frying pan or wok. Add shallots and garlic. Cook until shallots are just softened. Add cabbage and cook for a further 3-4 minutes. Add tomatoes and cook for another 3-4 minutes. Stir in the stock and simmer for 2 minutes.

In a large bowl beat the ricotta cheese and cream together. Add the drained pasta and toss to coat. Add the tomato mixture and toss again to coat the tagliatelle with the mixture. Serve immediately garnished with the grated cheese if you have chosen to use it.

Fast Lemon Chicken

This dish is delicious served with boiled rice or as an alternative you could serve with fresh egg noodles.

Ingredients

250g boneless chicken pieces
1 clove garlic
1 lemon
1 tablespoon plain flour
Small piece of ginger (optional)
250ml chicken stock
½ teaspoon caster sugar
1 egg yolk
2 tablespoons of olive oil
1 tablespoon fresh parsley or teaspoon dried parsley
Salt and pepper

Method

Grate the zest from the whole lemon then squeeze the juice from half and set aside. Peel and crush the garlic. Put flour, lemon zest and garlic in a bowl and mix thoroughly. Cut the chicken into bite sized pieces and toss in the flour mixture until well coated. Cover and leave to stand for 5 minutes.

Heat the oil in a large pan or wok. Add the chicken and cook over a medium heat for 5-8 minutes until the chicken is golden brown.

Peel and grate the ginger and stir into pan with any remaining flour, the stock and sugar. Bring to the boil and cook for a further 5 minutes until the chicken is tender and the sauce is reduced.

Blend the egg and lemon juice and add to the pan stirring all the time until the sauce thickens. Stir in the parsley. Taste, season to your liking and serve with boiled rice.

Note: To cook the perfect, fluffy rice use 1 measure of rice to 2 measures of water. Bring to boil, cover and simmer until the water is absorbed, stirring occasionally. That's it – perfect fluffy rice every time!

Crispy Turkey Rolls

A very satisfying and economical supper dish. Nice served with new potatoes and green salad.

Ingredients

1 boneless turkey breast fillet
25g gruyere cheese
Small slice ham
1 tablespoon plain flour
50g wholemeal breadcrumbs
1 egg
Salt and pepper
Vegetable oil for frying

Method

Chop the gruyere cheese and ham into small pieces and put onto flattened turkey breast fillet. Roll carefully to fully enclose the filling. Cut the roll into 2 inch pieces. You may need to secure with a cocktail stick whilst you fry your turkey rolls.

Put the flour and breadcrumbs onto separate plates. Season the flour. Beat the eggs in a shallow bowl.

Coat the turkey rolls in the seasoned flour, then coat in the beaten egg then roll in the breadcrumbs. For a crispier turkey roll, repeat the rolling in the egg then the breadcrumbs.

Place on tray, cover with clingfilm and chill for at least 30 minutes.

Heat the oil in a large pan. Add the breadcrumb coated turkey rolls and cook over a medium to high heat until golden, turning just once. Try not to move the rolls around the pan too much or you may lose the breadcrumb coating.

Remove from pan, drain on kitchen paper then serve immediately.

Fast Fish Curry

You can make this fish curry as hot as you like it – one of the perks of cooking for one!

Ingredients

1 small onion
1 clove garlic
150g small tomatoes
200g any skinless fish
20g flour
1 tablespoon vegetable oil
¾ dessertspoon of curry paste – as hot or mild as you prefer
50ml fish or vegetable stock
1 tablespoon fresh coriander to garnish
Seasoning

Method

Peel and finely chop the onion. Peel and crush the garlic. Halve the tomatoes. Cut your chosen fish into 4cm dice. Put the flour onto flat plate and season. Toss the fish in the seasoned flour until fully coated. Put any excess flour to one side.

Heat half the oil in a frying pan over a high heat. Add the fish and fry until golden on all sides. Remove from pan.

Heat remaining oil and add the onion and curry paste and fry for 3 minutes, stirring all the time. Return fish and any reserved flour to pan. Stir in tomatoes and stock. Bring to the boil and simmer for 5 minutes until fish is fully cooked.

Garnish with coriander and serve. Delicious served with warmed naan bread.

Hearty Sausage Casserole

A lovely one-dish winter warmer. You can add any vegetables to this casserole; the ingredient list is really just a suggestion.

Ingredients

1 small onion
1 clove garlic
1 rasher thick cut bacon
2 pork sausages
½ can chopped tomatoes
150ml chicken stock
1 bay leaf
2 teaspoons plain flour
Black pepper
Handful of frozen peas or butter beans

Method

Peel and finely slice the onion and crush the garlic. Chop the bacon into small pieces. Prick sausages with a fork and fry over a medium high heat in a non-stick pan. Turn regularly until nicely browned. Remove sausages from pan. Add garlic, onion and bacon and fry in the sausage fat over medium heat for 3 minutes until onions are softened. Add flour and stir well.

Cut each sausage into bite sized pieces and return to pan. Add stock, tomatoes and bay leaf. Season with the black pepper and bring to the boil to thicken the sauce. Reduce heat and simmer for about 15 minutes, stirring occasionally.

Add the peas or butter beans and simmer for another 5 minutes. Taste and adjust seasoning to your liking.

Serve with either a jacket potato or some creamy mashed potatoes.

Meatballs in the Hole

This is a twist on the classic 'Toad-in-the-Hole' (I've always wondered why that dish is called 'Toad-in-the-Hole'...). You can use any type of minced (ground) meat to make your meatballs and add any finely chopped herbs that take your fancy.

Ingredients

200g minced beef or lamb or pork etc.
1 small onion
1 clove garlic
1 teaspoon tomato puree or dessertspoon of tomato ketchup
1 dessertspoon of breadcrumbs
1 beaten egg
Oil for frying
Small handful of Herbs if desired

For the Batter

50g plain flour
1 egg
50ml milk
Seasoning

Method

Peel and finely chop the onion and garlic. Heat the oil and fry the onion and garlic until soft and transparent. Remove from pan and allow to cool slightly.

Put minced meat, tomato puree, breadcrumbs, herbs, cooked onion and garlic in a large bowl. Combine the ingredients well.

Add enough of the beaten egg to bind your mixture together.

Roll into small balls. To stop the meatballs sticking to your hands while you are rolling them, wet your hands with cold water.

Cook in a frying pan over a medium heat, rolling them around frequently until the meatballs are cooked and nicely brown.

Meanwhile whisk together flour, egg and a dash of the milk. Then add the rest of the milk until a smooth batter is achieved. Season.

Put a tablespoon of vegetable oil in a heatproof baking dish and place in hot oven until the oil is smoking hot. Remove the dish carefully and pour in the batter. Place your cooked meatballs in the batter.

Return to the oven and cook in the center of oven until the batter is risen and golden – about 200° C Gas mark 6. This will take around 15-20 minutes but keep an eye on it. Don't be tempted to open the door as the batter will drop – watch through the glass on the oven door.

Serve immediately with some nice gravy.

Note: If you make more meatballs than you need for this dish, you can freeze them uncooked and save for later. You could whip up a quick tomato sauce to serve with the meatballs.

Suitable for Vegetarian

Individual Sweet Onion and Goats Cheese Tarts

These individual tarts are ideal for a quick and easy supper served with a green salad or a few boiled new potatoes. They look like you have spent ages making them so are great to produce when you have company. Honestly – ANYONE can make these in minutes!

Ingredients

Packet of shortcrust or puff pastry (or you could make your own)
Jar of sweet onion chutney
Goat's cheese – easiest if you buy the goat's cheese in a roll.
Parsley to garnish
Small tart tins

Method

Lightly grease your tart tins.

Roll out your pastry to the thickness of a coin and line each tart tin carefully. Cover with greaseproof paper and fill with baking beans or dried peas to stop the pastry from rising (called baking blind). Cook in a pre-heated oven 180° until the edges are just beginning to brown.

Remove from oven and allow to cool slightly.

Cut goat's cheese into circles (if you bought a roll) or bite sized pieces. Take a spoonful of the onion chutney and spread over the base of your tart then put the goat's cheese on top. Add a little more onion chutney to the top of the cheese; you could also add a few slices of tomato if you like. Return to oven to bake – about 8-10 minutes.

You can serve these either hot or cold with a little chopped parsley sprinkled over each.

Note: If you don't have any tart tins you could simply cut your pastry into small squares and pinch the four corners so they stand up. Small squares will work better in this case. Then bake blind and fill as before.

Cheesy Stuffed Potato Skins

Again another very simple dish. The only problem you will face is choosing what to stuff the potato skins with if you want to ring the changes. But for the purpose of this recipe we will concentrate on the cheesy filling.

Ingredients

2 medium sized potatoes
Cream cheese
Small onion
Butter
1 tablespoon of oil
1 clove garlic if desired
Grated cheese.

Method

Place the potatoes in the microwave and cook until nearly soft inside. Next place in a hot oven to complete the baking and crisp the skins.

Meanwhile, chop the onion and garlic (if used) and fry in the oil until soft and transparent. Drain way any excess oil.

Remove potatoes from oven and, using a sharp knife, cut in half lengthways. Being careful with the hot potatoes, scoop the insides of the potatoes out into a bowl. Add the butter, onion, garlic and a handful of grated cheese. Mash together well.

Place the empty skins on a lightly greased baking tray and spread a little cream cheese over the inside of each skin.

Fill each skin with the cheesy potato mixture and top with a sprinkling of grated cheese. You could also add a slice of tomato or a sprinkling of chopped chives to the top of each at this stage.

Return to oven and bake until the cheese is melted and golden brown. Serve with a crisp green salad.

Spicy Chorizo Omelet

Another great omelet served with a few French fries or salad. My kids loved this with baked beans.

Ingredients

½ spicy chorizo sausage
2 eggs
½ teaspoon paprika
Knob of butter
Salt and pepper

Method

Thinly slice the chorizo sausage and whisk the eggs thoroughly. Add paprika, salt and pepper to the eggs.

Heat the butter in a small frying pan and add the chorizo. Fry over a medium to low heat for about 4 minutes until the slices are hot and just beginning to crisp.

Pour the egg mixture over the chorizo sausage. Allow to cook slowly until the egg is set and browning underneath. Place under the grill to brown the top of your omelet.

Serve immediately.

Homemade Sausage Patties

With all the bad press that shop bought sausages have been receiving, it is good to have the option to make your own.

If you make your own sausages you can experiment with different flavors by adding herbs and vegetables to your chosen meat. Sausages do not have to be made from pork but can be made using any meat you choose. Below is my own favorite sausage recipe.

Ingredients

250g of minced (ground) pork
1 apple or 1 pear
½ tsp fennel
½ tsp thyme
¼ tsp garlic
Salt and pepper
Olive oil for frying

Method

Peel, core and chop the apple (or pear).

Combine all the ingredients in a bowl and mix by hand until all your ingredients are well combined. Heat the oil in a frying pan on a low to medium heat.

Shape the sausage mixture into flat patties and cook for about 5-7mins on each side.

Place each patty on a paper towel over a plate to absorb any excess oil.

Serve with scrambled eggs, mushrooms and tomatoes.

Any excess sausage patties will freeze for later use.

Chicken with Leek Sauce

This is a lovely chicken dish and is quick and easy to prepare.

Ingredients

1 boneless chicken breast
1 large leek
30g butter
1 clove garlic
1 tablespoon wholegrain mustard
Small glass dry white wine
2 tablespoons crème fraiche

Method

Peel and crush the garlic. Trim leeks and cut into 1cm thick slices.

Melt the butter in a pan and add the garlic and chicken. Fry the chicken on both sides until it is a nice golden brown. Stir in the leeks, mustard and wine.

Bring the mixture to the boil adding a little water if necessary. Reduce the heat, cover and simmer for around 20 minutes or until the chicken is cooked.

Stir the crème fraiche into the pan. Taste and season to your liking. Serve immediately with some creamy mashed potatoes.

Note: When using wine in cooking, only use wine that you would drink yourself. If you wouldn't drink a glass of it yourself, it would not improve in any dish.

Pancakes with Chicken Stuffing

This is yet another recipe that will allow you to ring the changes with your fillings.

Ingredients

100g skinless cooked chicken meat (you could substitute chicken for mushrooms)
50g grated cheddar cheese
1 leek
20g butter
20g flour
150ml milk
Seasoning
3 ready-made pancakes or tortillas

Method

Cut the chicken into bite sized pieces and cut leek into thin slices.

Melt the butter in a saucepan, add the leek and fry for a couple of minutes until just softened. If using mushrooms instead of chicken you should fry the mushrooms with the leek.

Sprinkle in the flour and stir gently to coat the leeks. Add the milk in gradually stirring all the time whilst the mixture thickens. Add half the cheese and stir until melted before adding the chicken.

Cook for about 5 minutes or until chicken is cooked through. Taste and season to your liking.

Preheat the grill. Spoon the chicken sauce along the center of each pancake and roll up to enclose the filling. Transfer to a shallow ovenproof dish and sprinkle over the remaining cheese. Grill for 3-4 minutes or until golden brown.

Serve immediately with a crunchy green salad dressed with a lemon vinaigrette.

Tomato Noodles with Pesto and Bacon

Quick and easy supper dish that is a personal favorite of mine.

Ingredients

125g noodles of your choice. You can use fettucine, spaghetti, tagliatelle etc.
2 tablespoons olive oil
200g cherry tomatoes
1 clove garlic
2 tablespoons green pesto (from a jar or your own home-made)
1 rasher bacon
Salt
Watercress for garnish (you could use grated parmesan cheese if you prefer)

Method

Add the pasta and 1 tablespoon oil to a pan of boiling water and cook according to pasta packet instructions.

Halve the tomatoes, peel and finely chop the garlic and cut bacon into bite sized pieces.

Heat the remaining oil in a wok or pan. Add garlic and bacon, frying until bacon is cooked. Add tomatoes and cook for 5 minutes until tomatoes are lightly browned and softened. Taste and season.

Drain the pasta thoroughly and return to pan. Add the pesto and toss to coat. Pour into a large serving dish and tip the tomato and bacon mixture over the top of the pasta. Garnish with watercress or parmesan and serve immediately.

Vegetable, Rice and Pesto Salad

This is a very tasty way to use up any leftover vegetables that you have sitting in your fridge. You could also add any leftover cold meat to the salad if you like. This salad is a great picnic dish or as an accompaniment to a steak.

The vegetables listed below are simply suggestions; use whatever you have available.

Ingredients

120g long grain rice
120g cherry tomatoes
Red pepper
Green pepper
Spring onions
Few slices of cucumber
1 clove garlic
Tablespoon pesto
Tablespoon white wine vinegar
2 tablespoons good olive oil
Seasoning

Method

Rinse the rice and cook using the 2 to 1 method (2 parts water to 1 part rice). Drain the rice and rinse under cold running water. Transfer to your chosen serving bowl.

Chop your vegetables into small dice. Mix into the rice thoroughly.

Peel and crush the clove of garlic. Add the garlic to the pesto, white wine vinegar and olive oil. Whisk until well combined. Drizzle the dressing over the rice salad and toss. Serve immediately.

Creamy Courgettes with Spaghetti

Ingredients

1 courgette
1 clove garlic
Parmesan cheese
1 tablespoon olive oil
150g dried spaghetti
1 dessertspoon crème fraiche
1 dessertspoon fresh shredded basil leaves
Black pepper

Method

Slice the courgettes and peel and crush the garlic. Grate or thinly slice the parmesan cheese.

Heat half the oil in a frying pan and add the courgettes and garlic. Cook for 3-4 minutes stirring occasionally.

Meanwhile cook the spaghetti as per the packet instructions. Drain well then add to the courgette. Add the remaining oil and the crème fraiche and toss well. Taste and season to your liking. Serve topped with parmesan cheese.

Potato Crisps with Lemon and Lime Salsa

A great supper snack. Great to eat in front of the TV with an assortment of dips. The crisps will keep if kept in an airtight container.

Ingredients

For the Salsa:

200g ripe tomatoes
Half small onion
1 clove garlic
1 tablespoon fresh coriander
Juice of half lemon
Juice of half lime
1 tablespoon good olive oil
1 teaspoon balsamic vinegar
Chopped chili (optional)
Seasoning

For the Crisps:

Waxy potatoes – as many as you want!
Vegetable oil to deep fry
Salt

Method

To make the Salsa:

Make a cross in the top of each tomato, put in a bowl and pour boiling water over them. Soak for 2 minutes then peel. Remove seeds and chop roughly. Chop onion and coriander.

Mix onion, tomatoes, lime and lemon juice, vinegar, chili (if used), garlic and oil together well. Chill for at least 15 minutes before serving.

To make the Crisps:

Peel the potatoes and slice very thinly. Soak the slices in iced water for at least 15 minutes. Drain and dry thoroughly on a clean tea towel. Half fill a deep pan with the vegetable oil and heat until a cube of bread turns brown in 30 seconds when dropped in. *Carefully* lower the potato slices into the oil a few at a time and deep fry turning frequently, until the slices rise to the top and are golden brown. Remove crisps and drain on kitchen paper. Sprinkle with a little salt. When cold store in an airtight container until you are ready to use.

Note: There are lots of variations for delicious dips to eat with your crisps. Be adventurous and invent one of your own.

Italian Style Pork Chops

Pork is a very reasonably price meat and can be very tasty if not overcooked. This recipe is simple to make and adds a bit of an Italian flavor to your meal for a change. It is delicious served with boiled potatoes or just chunks of crusty bread.

Ingredients

2 lean pork chops
1 tablespoon olive oil
1 small onion
2 cloves garlic
1 tablespoon chopped fresh rosemary
1 teaspoon grated lemon zest
1 dessertspoon finely chopped oregano
100ml chicken stock
Half can of chopped tomatoes
Seasoning

Method

Trim any excess fat from the chops. Heat the oil in a frying pan and cook chops for about 2 minutes on each side or until nicely browned. Remove from pan.

Peel and finely chop the onion and cook until soft and transparent. Peel and crush the garlic and add to the onions with the chopped rosemary, oregano and lemon zest. Cook for around 2 minutes.

Reduce the heat and return the chops to the pan along with the stock and tomatoes. Simmer over a low heat for 10-12 minutes or until the chops are cooked through and the sauce is slightly thickened. Remove from the heat, taste and season to your liking.

Irish Style Lamb Stew

This classic dish is a nourishing meal in itself and is particularly good served with fresh crusty bread.

Ingredients

1 clove garlic
120g onions
250g small new potatoes
2 small carrots
1 tablespoon oil
200g diced lean lamb (frozen is fine)
10g plain flour
200ml stock (lamb or beef)
Half teaspoon dried thyme
1 bay leaf
1 dessertspoon chopped fresh flat-leaf parsley
Seasoning

Method

Peel and crush the garlic. Peel and finely slice the onions and carrots. Wash the potatoes and cut any large ones in half.

Heat the oil in a pan and add the lamb and garlic. Fry for around 5 minutes turning often until the meat is browned all over. Drain off any excess fat and sprinkle the flour over the lamb. Stir for around 1 minute.

Add onions, carrots and stock to the pan. Bring to the boil stirring constantly until the liquid thickens. Add the thyme and bay leaf. Cover and simmer over a low heat for around 10 minutes. Add the potatoes and cook for a further 15-20 minutes or until both the meat and potatoes are tender.

Taste and season to your liking, add the parsley for garnish and serve. Delicious, comforting dish!

Almond Pesto and Pasta

Quick, tasty and simple to make, this pasta dish is great either on its own or served with a tomato salad.

Ingredients

125g dried spaghetti
1 clove garlic
75g blanched almonds
10g fresh basil leaves
3 tablespoons olive oil
Grated parmesan cheese

Method

Cook spaghetti as per the packet instruction being careful not to overcook.

Peel the garlic. Dry fry the nuts in a frying pan for 3-4 minutes tossing until golden brown. Reserve 20g of the nuts and put the rest in a food processor. Add the garlic, basil (keeping a few leaves back), oil and cheese. Blend for a few seconds until smooth.

Drain the pasta and return to the pan. Add the almond pesto and toss until the pasta is coated with the sauce.

Using a sharp knife, chop the remaining almonds and sprinkle over the pasta. Taste and season to your liking. Garnish with the reserved basil leaves. Serve immediately with hot garlic bread.

Note: You could add some chopped cooked chicken or a handful of prawns to this dish if you like.

Easy Chicken and Coconut Curry

Ingredients

Half of 400ml can coconut milk (the other half can be used for Parsnip and Coconut Soup)
Small bunch coriander
2 large garlic cloves
Small piece fresh root ginger
1 green chili
1 tablespoon olive oil
4 skinless chicken thighs or drumsticks
1 small onion, finely chopped
Small piece of cinnamon stick
1 tsp cumin powder
1 tsp coriander powder
1 tsp Garam masala

Method

Blend the coconut milk and coriander in a food processor, then tip out and set aside. Put the garlic, ginger and chili into the food processor, and blend with enough water to make a paste.

Heat the oil in a large pan. Brown the chicken well then remove. Add the onion and cinnamon and fry until golden. Add the chili paste to the pan and cook until most of the liquid has evaporated.

Return the chicken and stir in the powdered spices plus the coconut milk and coriander paste. Bring to a boil, cover and cook for 30-40 minutes, remove the lid halfway through to thicken the sauce.

Check the chicken is cooked, season to taste adding a splash of water if the sauce has thickened too much.

Satisfying Beef Stew

This stew is delicious due to its long cooking time. The shin beef just falls apart. Lovely to come home to when cooked in a slow cooker.

Ingredients

250g diced shin beef
1 tablespoon olive oil
1 small onion finely chopped
1 clove of garlic crushed
1 carrot chopped
1 stick of celery chopped
1 tablespoon sundried tomato paste
1 x 400g tin chopped tomatoes
400ml beef stock
1 bay leaf

Method

Pre-heat the oven to 170°C. Heat the oil in a large pan. Add the shin beef and brown on all sides.

Add the onion, garlic, carrot and celery. Sweat for 10 minutes.

Stir in the tomato puree, then add the tinned tomatoes, beef stock and bay leaf.

Bring to the boil. Put into a casserole dish and seal with foil. Put in the oven for 2 to 3 hours until the shin beef is very tender. Or transfer to a slow cooker and leave to cook on medium setting until needed.

Serve with steamed cabbage, broccoli, cauliflower, creamy mashed potatoes or just a chunk of crusty bread.

Note: You can substitute the shin beef for pork, chicken or turkey if you prefer.

Simple Chicken Casserole

This casserole has been a great standby for when unexpected guests arrived, I simply increased the recipe according to the number of guests. But it is just as simple to make for one person.

Ingredients

1 chicken fillet
1 small red onion
3 large mushrooms
150ml passatta or chopped tinned tomatoes
1 tsp dried mixed herbs
1 tablespoon olive oil
Salt and pepper

Method

Heat the olive oil in a frying pan. Chop the onion in to a rough dice and add to the pan. Stir-fry until golden.

Add the chicken fillet to the pan and brown on both sides.

Thinly slice the mushrooms and add these along with the dried herbs to the pan. Stir-fry until golden.

Add the passatta, bring to a gentle simmer and allow to cook until the chicken is cooked through, approximately 15 minutes. If the pan starts to dry out add some cold water.

Taste and season to your liking. Serve with green vegetables or crusty bread.

Cauliflower Cheese with Bacon

This dish is delicious either on its own or as a side dish with a thick slice of cold ham and a few new potatoes.

Ingredients

10 cauliflower florets
1 rasher back bacon
Seasoning

For the sauce:

30g butter
30g flour
Milk
Grated cheese

Method

Cook the cauliflower florets in lightly seasoned water until tender. Drain and arrange in ovenproof dish. Cut the bacon into small dice and fry until crispy. Set aside.

For the sauce.

Melt the butter in a saucepan over a medium heat then add the flour stirring continuously with a wooden spoon. It will look lumpy at first but it will come together; so don't panic!

Once the flour and butter are mixed together to a paste, begin to add the milk a bit at a time, stirring all the time. The mixture will thicken each time you add milk. Keep adding more milk until your sauce is at your desired thickness (I like mine quite thick). Add as much grated cheese as you like until it tastes good to you. Stir in the crispy bacon. Taste and season.

Pour your sauce over the cooked cauliflower and sprinkle a little grated cheese over the top. Put under the grill until golden brown. Serve immediately.

Note: If you want to make this in advance, don't grill the dish but cover and chill. When you want to use it, put in a pre-heated oven until the top is golden brown.

| Suitable for Vegetarian | *Vegetable Frittata* |

You could add bacon to this frittata to make a great dish for the non-vegetarian.

Ingredients (these are really just suggestions, you can use any leftover vegetables)

Broccoli split into florets
1 spring onion
Green beans
Courgette
Handful frozen peas
Handful frozen corn kernels
2 eggs
1 tablespoon olive oil
Parmesan cheese (optional)
Seasoning

Method

Pre-heat the grill to its highest setting. Chop vegetables and cook in lightly salted water for a few minutes then drain well and dry off on kitchen paper.

Heat the oil in a frying pan and sauté the drained vegetables for a few minutes.

Pour the beaten eggs into the pan, drawing the egg from the sides into the center, until set underneath.

Sprinkle with grated Parmesan and finish under the grill until the top is set and a lovely golden brown. Serve immediately.

Courgette and Cod Fritters

Ingredients

1 egg
50g cod
½ courgette grated
Handful grated cheese
Seasoning
Olive oil
Small knob of butter

Method

Cut the cod into small, bite sized pieces. Whisk the egg well and add the cod, grated courgette, grated cheese (if used) and salt and pepper to taste. Mix until well combined.

Heat 2 tablespoons of olive oil in a frying pan. Drop spoonfuls of the mixture into the pan and cook for around 4 minutes on each side. Towards the end of cooking, add the butter and spoon over the fritters to glaze.

These are delicious served with a crisp green salad.

Five Minute Honey Pork and Pepper Stir Fry

A stir fry is one of the quickest and easiest dishes to prepare – it takes longer to chop the ingredients than it does to cook. The great thing about a stir fry is that you can use all your leftovers to create a delicious meal. The list of ingredients below is just a suggestion – you can use whatever combination you prefer.

Ingredients

100g boneless pork
1 spring onion
1 red pepper
Handful mange tout
Handful green beans
Pak choi
1 tablespoon water or stock
1 tablespoon runny honey
1 tablespoon sesame oil
Seasoning

Method

Cut the pork into thin strips. Cut your pepper or your choice of vegetables into small pieces.

Heat the sesame oil in a wok or frying pan. Add the pork and stir fry for 2 minutes. Add the vegetables and stir fry for a further 1-2 minutes leaving pak choi until the last minute. Add the water or stock. Stir fry for a further minute until the water has gone. Stir in the honey and toss to coat everything. Taste and season if required. Serve immediately.

Note: A stir fry is one dish where you can really let your imagination loose. You can use any ingredients you fancy as long as they are chopped to approximately the same size. You could add a dash of white wine vinegar to the above dish to create a sweet and sour stir fry.

Sweet Lambs Liver and Mushrooms

Liver is a meat you either love or hate but, if you have never tried it, this dish is a great introduction to a cheap and nutritious meat.

Ingredients

200g Lambs Liver
3 tablespoons milk
Small red onion
100g mushrooms (any type)
1 tablespoon oil
2 tablespoons plain flour
2 tablespoons redcurrant jelly
2 tablespoons lamb or beef stock
Parsley for garnish
Seasoning

Method

Trim the liver and slice into strips. Put in a bowl with the milk and set aside for 10 minutes. This helps to make the liver tender and removes any strong flavors before cooking. Peel and finely slice the onion and mushrooms.

Heat the oil in a non-stick frying pan and add the onion. Fry for around two minutes or until softened. Add the mushrooms and cook for another two minutes.

Meanwhile put the flour on a flat plate. Drain and dry the liver, discarding the milk. Coat the liver in the flour and add to the pan. Cook over a high heat for 2-3 minutes until liver is browned on all sides. Stir in the redcurrant jelly and stock. Bring to the boil and simmer for just 1 minute.

Taste and season if required. Serve immediately. This is very tasty served on a bed of fresh egg noodles.

Ham Hash with a Kick

This is a great way to use up leftover potato and ham. You could substitute the ham for fish if you prefer.

Ingredients

1 onion
250g cooked, floury potatoes
100g cooked, lean ham
30g butter
1 tablespoon chili oil
1 teaspoon tabasco sauce
1 tablespoon chopped parsley
Seasoning

Method

Peel and slice the onion. Cut potatoes into small dice.

Melt 20g of the butter in a frying pan and add the onion.

Fry gently until softened but not browned, around 2-3 minutes.

Add the chili oil and potatoes. Fry for around 7-8 minutes, turning occasionally until crisp and lightly browned.

Add the ham and remaining 10g of butter and cook for a further 2 minutes or until the ham is heated through.

Stir in the tabasco sauce, taste and season if required. Serve immediately. Delicious topped with a lightly poached egg.

Sweet and Sour Minced Pork

This is a good way to use up any leftover pineapple. Pineapples are really cheap at the moment and can be used for some delicious desserts as well as added to a lot of savory dishes.

Ingredients

200g minced pork
50g pineapple cut into chunks
Small can of sliced peaches, drained
1 small onion
1 clove garlic
1 yellow pepper
1 tablespoon oil
1 dessertspoon red wine vinegar
1 tablespoon light soy sauce
1 tablespoon clear honey
1 tablespoon tomato puree (tomato ketchup will do)
Few fresh oregano leaves (optional)

Method

Peel and finely chop the onion, peel and crush the garlic clove. Deseed and finely slice the pepper.

Heat the oil in a frying pan and add the onion, garlic and peppers and cook for around 5 minutes or until softened. Add the pork and cook over a high heat until browned, stirring all the time to prevent the meat from catching. Drain off any excess fat.

Add the vinegar, light soy sauce and tomato puree. Stir in 100 ml water until well combined. Cover and simmer for around 15 minutes.

Add pineapple and peaches and cook for a further 5 minutes adding more water if required. Chop oregano (if using) and sprinkle over before serving. Delicious served with rice.

Parsnip and Coconut Soup

This soup is a great standby to have in the fridge for when you need a quick supper. As this recipe only uses half a can of coconut milk, you can use the leftover milk in the 'Chicken Skewers with Satay Sauce' recipe on the next page.

Ingredients

3 parsnips
1 clove garlic
Half a can of coconut milk
Seasoning

Method

Peel and chop the parsnips into small chunks. Boil in salted water until soft. Drain well. Put the parsnips into a blender along with the crushed garlic and coconut milk. Blend until smooth adding extra milk if the soup is too thick.

Reheat and serve with buttered crusty bread.

Chicken Skewers with Satay Sauce

Homemade chicken skewers are much nicer than those you would get from a takeaway and really simple to make.

Ingredients

1 skinless chicken breast
1 dessertspoon olive oil
1 dessertspoon lemon juice

For the Satay Sauce

50g smooth peanut butter
1 dessertspoon olive oil
1 dessertspoon hot water
1 dessertspoon light soy sauce
1 tablespoon apple juice
1 tablespoon coconut milk

Method

To make the satay sauce simply mix all your ingredients together.

Soak 4 wooden skewers in water for at least 15 minutes to prevent burning.

Cut the chicken breast into 4 strips lengthways. Thread each strip onto a skewer. Mix the oil and lemon juice together and brush over the chicken.

Preheat the grill and cook the skewers until the chicken is cooked and golden brown all over. Serve hot with the satay sauce.

Tomato Stuffed Peppers

Stuffed peppers are a great standby for if you have unexpected visitors. They take just minutes to prepare and look like you have gone to a lot of trouble. Delicious served with a crisp green salad or a few French fries.

Ingredients

1 Pepper – any color
Cooked rice
2 tomatoes
1 clove garlic
Fresh basil leaves
1 shallot
1 tablespoon oil
Grated cheese

Method

Cut top off the pepper and reserve for later. Scoop out the seeds and white core from the body of the pepper then blanch the pepper and top in boiling water for around 2 minutes. Remove and drain well.

Heat half the oil in a frying pan and add the crushed garlic and finely chopped shallot. Cook for a couple of minutes until the shallot is transparent. Chop the tomatoes and add to the shallot and garlic. Cook for a further 3 minutes. If you are using any other vegetables you should add them at this stage.

Remove from the heat and stir in the cooked rice, cheese and basil leaves. Mix together well, taste and season to your liking.

Place your peppers in an oven-proof dish and fill with the rice mixture. Top with a little grated cheese before placing the top on the pepper. Drizzle with a little oil, loosely cover with foil and bake in a medium to hot oven for around 30 minutes or until cooked.

Some Simple Conversion Figures

Oven Temperatures

°C	°F	Gas
110	225	¼
120	250	½
140	275	1
160	325	3
180	350	4
200	400	6
220	425	7
240	475	9

Remember to always preheat your oven to the desired temperature.

Weights

1oz (ounce)	=	28g (gram)
1lb (pound)	=	454g
2.2046 lbs	=	1kg (kilo)

Liquid

1 fl oz	=	25 ml
3½ fl oz	=	100 ml
8 fl oz	=	250 ml
1 pint	=	600 ml
1¾ pints	=	1 ltr

Thank You

Thank you for buying this book and I really hope it has given you some inspiration for simple, economical and interesting meals to prepare for yourself. Remember, most of these recipes can be adapted to your personal taste by adding your own favorite ingredients. So be adventurous and change things around a bit – this is how family favorite recipes are actually born.

If you enjoyed this book I would really appreciate it if you would leave a review on Amazon. Simply type in the title and author in the search bar of Amazon and click on the book and leave your review. Thank you so much.

If you are interested in receiving notification of the next book in the 'Budget Cooking for One' series, please leave your email address at the address below.

www.eepurl.com/SZOLH

If you have any simple recipes for one that you would like to contribute to my next book, please email me.

Penelope.Oates21@gmail.com

Upcoming Books in the 'Budget Cooking for One' series:

Crockpot Cooking for One
Simple Desserts for One
TV Snacks for One
Chicken Recipes for One
Vegetarian Cooking for One

Thank you again.

Penny

Notes

Made in the USA
San Bernardino, CA
17 December 2014